The Holy Grail of Public Leadership

Public Leadership

(and the Never-Ending Quest for Measurable Impact)

Tony —
Thanks for the
getting the bills
paid.

— adam

The Holy Grail of Public Leadership
(and the Never-Ending Quest for Measurable Impact)

Adam Luecking

Foreword by Michael McAfee, Ed.D.

Edited by Olivier Kamanda

Published by
Fourth Quadrant Publishing
Rockville, MD 20852
www.fourthquadrantpublishing.com

To order additional books go to www.resultsleadership.org

ISBN: 9780615792897

Library of Congress Control Number: 2013937250

Contributors:
Rolf Grafwallner, Sara Morgan Evans,
Susan Brutschy and Deanna Zachary, Molly McGrath,
Louisa McKay, Ruth Jordan and Vicki Myson

Short Essays Editing by Adaora Otiji
Layout by Ross A. Feldner

Special thanks to Phil Lee and Mark Friedman for inspiring the journey, to Justin Miklas for the adventure, to my dad for introducing me to the concept of the never-ending quest at a very young age, to my mom for keeping me on the right path, and to my beautiful wife and kids for making it all worthwhile.

Table of Contents

Foreword

At a young age I knew I wanted to improve the quality of life for those living in poverty. Fortunately, I was able to pursue my purpose as soon as I graduated from college. I joined a community foundation and set out on a course to change the world. There was just one problem. I was focused on "doing good" - not on getting results. After serving in the philanthropic, nonprofit and government sectors for more than seventeen years, I had grown weary of just doing good work. I longed to know if I was actually making a difference in the lives of poor children and families. Fortunately, at the height of my disillusionment I met Adam and his network of results-based leaders.

Adam helped me to understand how I could use Results-Based Accountability™ (RBA) to answer the question that was at the heart of my disillusionment - is anyone better off? While I could not answer the question on my own, the process of trying to answer it immediately reconnected me with my purpose, passion and leadership voice. This simple, yet elegant question launched me on a wonderful journey of personal and professional discovery. I began to focus all of my efforts on becoming a results-based leader. This journey led me to leave federal service and to focus my efforts on what I most cared about - improving the educational and development outcomes for poor children.

Today, as the Director of the Promise Neighborhoods Institute at PolicyLink, I'm able to use Adam's guidance to change the world! I'm finally able to connect my desire to "do good" with a measurable impact. I'm honored to lead a collaboration focused on ensuring that all children and youth grow up in communities of opportunity (we call them Promise Neighborhoods) and have access to great schools and strong systems of family and community support that prepare them to attain an excellent education and successfully transition to college and a career. While this vision is laudable, without results it's inadequate. Fortunately, we have ten results and twenty standard indicators that we're using to help neighborhoods measure their progress!

The Holy Grail of Public Leadership is the handbook that I use to guide my daily journey to making a measurable impact in the lives of the 13 million children living in poverty.

Michael A. McAfee, Ed.D.
Director
Promise Neighborhoods Institute at PolicyLink

The Holy Grail

Congratulations! You've taken the first step on a journey for one of mankind's most prized treasures. Wars have been fought over it. Heroes have given their lives searching for it. Its legend borders on myth. But you—just by reading this book—are one step closer to attaining the Holy Grail . . . of Public Leadership.

That's right. The Holy Grail of Public Leadership. But you won't find any references to Monty Python or Indiana Jones in this book. You will, find a treasure just as valuable as any in the Da Vinci Code.

The quest for the Holy Grail of Public Leadership puts individuals, community groups, and social sector organizations on the path to achieve Measurable Impact. For those in the public and non-profit sectors, Measur.able Impact is the Holy Grail of Public Leadership.

Measurable Impact is "beating the baseline" or "turning the curve" on a data trend line at both the community and organizational levels (see *Exhibit A* and some more examples found in *Appendix A*).

Measurable Impact is the difference between *promoting awareness about HIV/AIDS* and *lowering infection rates by 30 percent across the most vulnerable segment of a population; strengthening social engagement* and *doubling the number of registered voters in a non-election year; supporting our schools* and *raising the percentage of third graders proficient in reading.* It's the difference between poorly conceived, vague goals which leave those in need underserved and demonstrable change that improves the quality of people's lives.

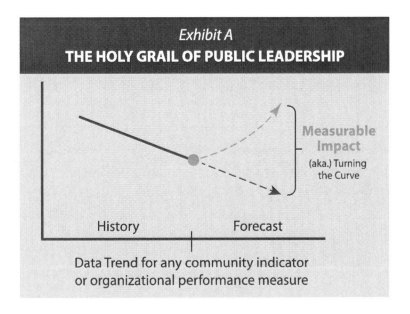

Achieving this goal is no easy task. Whether you're in the public sector or private sector, public service or public office, leadership for the greater good will test your patience. Here is what I have learned, and I bet you have experienced it too: new ideas always tend to sound better in your head than they read on paper. And putting them into practice is never quite as easy as your plan made it seem. You'll hold meetings about logistics. You'll hold meetings about resources. You'll hold meetings about how you hold too many meetings. During that time partnerships will come and go. Money goes and never comes. And even when you finally achieve the goal you've been working towards, you *have to start the process over again next year* because even the greatest accomplishments are quickly eclipsed by new challenges.

And in today's economic climate, service agencies and social organizations are being squeezed at both ends. State and local government budgets are tightening. Down economic times have slashed budgets for crucial public services across the board. That means less money for job training, health, housing, and education.

That same economic pressure also has a depressing effect on communities. Not only are our towns and cities struggling with smaller incomes, so are many families. The Brooking Institute's Metropolitan Policy Program study, "The Re-Emergence of Concentrated Poverty" found that over the first decade of the 2000s, "the poor population [grew] by 12.3 million, driving the total number of Americans in poverty to a historic high of 46.2 million." More people are in need of help than they have been in recent memory.

Don't tell people how to do things, tell them what to do and let them surprise you with their results.

George S. Patton

All of this means that leadership—*your* leadership—will be critical to carrying the day. Effective, meaningful leadership requires inspiring those around you to plan better, think clearer, move faster, and work smarter. Leaders have a responsibility to help create a culture that is conducive to change and Measurable Impact. Measurable Impact gives all those who share in the sacrifices of public service and nonprofit work the confidence that their work is making a quantifiable difference.

It won't happen overnight. In fact, it can't happen overnight. More than anything else this is a journey of self-development. As the saying goes, in order to change the world, you first have to change yourself.

That's why the metaphor of the quest for the Holy Grail is so applicable. Although the story varies among different cultures and religions, there are two elements common to all versions: the dedication and sacrifice that are part of the journey and the life-altering, transformative powers the Grail bestows that make all those sacrifices worthwhile.

We all have our personal quests and journeys—the drive to achieve our purpose. Find that desire to serve, heal, educate, train, organize, or whatever will motivate your journey.

I can't offer you a map because each journey is unique. But what I can offer is a compass, some milestones to aim for and traps to avoid, and some tools that will assist you in your quest. And that's what this book is all about. In these chapters, I'll discuss how to lead your organization and community (no matter what your job title) in the quest for Measurable Impact. This book will draw upon the Results Based Accountability™ ("RBA") framework developed by Mark Friedman and explained in his book, *Trying Hard is Not Enough*. But this book aims to do more than just instruct you on how to achieve change, it also intends to keep you focused along the way.

In Chapter 2, I'll identify the mental barriers that stall our progress and can even discourage us from our quest. Next, I'll introduce a set of vocabulary terms that will help you communicate more clearly about achieving measurable impact. Finally, I'll take a page from the RBA framework and illustrate how asking the right questions can help avoid common pitfalls.

Once you're on your way, Chapter 3 will explain how to engage others to take part in this quest with you to improve your community. Here, I'll focus on the fundamentals of leadership to change the community's culture, resources to fund your operations, and communication to let others know what you've achieved and where you still need to go.

In Chapter 4, you'll pick up the tools to develop your organization to reach its full potential. You have big goals, so you're going to need a strong team to make things happen. Start by recruiting the right people and cutting the dead weight. Invest in coaching, training, and personal development. Practice. Keep practicing. Practice some more. Market your value. And celebrate your success. Get coached. Encourage personal development. By Chapter 5, you and your team will be focused, with clear goals in mind, and a plan to achieve them. The only remaining question is: will you be ready to reach that Measurable Impact? As you close in on your goal, make sure that you'll be able to identify success at every level: for the community, for each program, and for each individual that's contributing their time and talent to make progress possible.

If you're reading this book, it's because you believe in a cause: an unmet need, an un-seized opportunity, an unfulfilled goal. You may want to serve those on the outskirts of opportunity or see in your community a reflection of the values you hold most dear.

Whatever *it* is, *it* is worth fighting for. It's worth planning for. It's worth leading others who are willing to share in sacrifices of service and join you by aligning their efforts. The journey is long, but it's worth it. And all you need to do is take the first step.

Your Quest Begins

It's 5 am on the first day of your epic quest and the day dawns cold and crisp. Over the horizon rain seeps from the lining of low-hanging clouds, just barely breaking the stillness of the night. It's grey and wet and dreary. Only the most dedicated people in the world are up early on a day like this: Olympic marathon runners, fugitives on the lam, Navy Seals, and you—the most motivated of them all.

But you're still a little groggy. So you hit the snooze button and buy yourself another five minutes. And then you think: *my bathrobe is still in the washing machine, which means a long, chilly walk to the shower. I might as well warm-up in bed a bit longer.* Snooze. *Didn't that staff meeting get postponed until 10:30 today? I'm sure no one will notice if I come in a little bit late. Who gets to work by 9 am, anyway?* Snooze Again. *It's not like we're actually going to get the funding to move forward before tomorrow.* More snooze.

Finally, rather than waking up at the crack of dawn, you're rolling out of bed at the crack of noon (Oh, and you missed the morning staff meeting too!).

Why did this happen?

"Anyone who has never made a mistake has never tried anything new"

Albert Einstein

Because there are plenty of reasons *not to get up in the morning:*

- monotonous routine;
- uninspiring co-workers;
- poor leadership;
- lack of purpose;
- lack of commitment;

- lack of money;
- lack of sleep;

and the list goes on.

But the only list you should be compiling at 5 am on a cold, wet day is a list of *reasons why today is a new opportunity to do better than yesterday:*

- to set an example for your kids;
- to shape a community that you can be proud of;
- to improve your organization;
- to teach someone a new skill;
- to get that raise;
- to get that promotion;
- to reverse a decline in living standards;
- to expand that recycling program into one more neighborhood;
- to promote awareness about the dangers of smoking;
- to change someone's life for the better;
- to help those who can't help themselves; or
- to create Measurable Impact.

and *that* list goes on, too.

The first step on this quest, is determining what Measurable Impact means to you. However you define it, it should excite you each morning, especially because you are your own best motivator.

After laying this mental foundation, the rest of the process becomes much easier. There will always be times when we fall short of our own expectations. But if we dwell on these shortcomings, we'll find it harder to overcome the next hurdle. Then we suffer from a lack of confidence. And the cycle begins all over again.

"If you think you're too small to have an impact, try going to bed with a mosquito"

Anita Roddick OBE

Here's a great example of what we should do instead:

We all know that Bruce Lee was one of the most successful, talented, and popular martial artists in the world. But he didn't achieve stardom with ease.

When he was twenty-eight years old, after being passed over for a series of movie and TV roles, with no savings to speak of, and a baby on the way, Lee wrote a letter to himself:

My Definite Chief Aim

I, Bruce Lee, will be the first highest paid Oriental super star in the United States. In return I will give the most exciting performances and render the best of quality in the capacity of an actor. Starting 1970 I will achieve world fame and from then onward till the end of 1980 I will have in my possession $10,000,000. I will live the way I please and achieve inner harmony and happiness.

Bruce Lee
1969

...and the rest is history.

You don't need to desire world fame and a $10 million bank account, to make the most of Bruce Lee's example. But his clear understanding of his own goals, as well as his discipline and motivation, no doubt played a role in achieving success. There's no reason why the same can't work for you too.

Once you know how to motivate yourself, you'll figure out how motivate and inspire others. It should come as no surprise that positive, purposeful affirmations are infectious. People like being around others who make them feel good. And we're more likely to work hard and collaborate effectively if we're in a positive, encouraging environment. I'll explore this further in Chapter 4.

Government agencies must learn to be clear about what they want to accomplish and not get stuck in the rut of doing what they have always done.

Shelley Metzenbaum,
White House Office of Management and Budget

As a leader, you have the opportunity (and the responsibility) to create this kind of environment. You will have to find ways to encourage others that the quest for Measurable Impact is a journey that's worth taking for them too.

The RBA framework mentioned is instructive here. It helps provide the core concepts and language that will sustain not only your efforts, but those of your organization, and the other stakeholders in the community.

First, we have to define a few key terms[1]:

Result: *a population condition of well-being for children, adults, families and communities, stated in plain language.* Results are conditions that voters and taxpayers can understand. They are about the well-being of people in a community, city, county, state, or nation. Examples include: Healthy Children, Children Ready for School, Children Succeeding in School, Families are Economically Secure, A Safe Community, and A Clean Environment.

Indicator: *a measure that helps quantify the achievement of a result.* Indicators answer the question, "How would we recognize this result if we fell over it?"

Strategy: *a coherent collection of actions that have a reasoned chance of improving results.* Strategies are made up of the best thinking about what works and include the contributions of many partners. Strategies operate at both the population and performance levels.

Performance Measure: *a measure of how well a program, agency or service system is working.* The most important performance measures tell us whether program customers are better off. These measures are considered as customer results to distinguish them from population results. RBA uses three types of performance measures:

1. How much we do?
2. How well did we do it?
3. Is anyone better off?

"Insanity: doing the same thing over and over again and expecting different results."

Albert Einstein

Results-Based Accountability™ , as the name suggests, argues that efforts to achieve results for a given population work best when stakeholders, agree on the desired end, understand their roles, and use data to mark their progress. It sounds complicated, but it's based on two simple principles:

1. Knowing where you want to end up will help determine the best way to get there; and
2. Using data-driven, transparent, and inclusive de-

cision-making will allow others to share in charting a path to achieve those results.

As Albert Einstein once noted, "no problem has ever been solved at the level of consciousness that created it." If I walk into my kitchen and see a puddle of water on the floor, I may have a problem, but I won't immediately know what kind of problem:

1. someone may have knocked over a glass;

2. there may be a leak from the ceiling; or

3. my dog may have had an accident.

I could mop it up, but that won't really solve my problem. What I should be doing is asking questions. Is there broken glass? Is there a hole in my ceiling? Have I taken my dog Lucy out for a walk today?

It's only when we ask the right questions *and get the right answers* that we can zero in on solving our problem and meeting our challenge. You wouldn't pack for vacation without finding out about the weather, so why would you try to save the world before asking critical questions about the problem you're trying to solve?

RBA tells us that there are two sets of questions we need to wrestle with at the outset of our journey for Measurable Impact: (1) questions about the population we hope to affect and (2) questions about the program performance we hope to affect.

The Seven Population Accountability Questions	The Seven Performance Accountability Questions
1. What are the quality of life conditions we want for the children, adults and families who live in our community?	1. Who are our customers?
2. What would these conditions look like if we could see them?	2. How can we measure if our customers are better off?
3. How can we measure these conditions?	3. How can we measure if we are delivering services well?
4. How are we doing on the most important of these measures?	4. How are we doing on the most important of these measures?
5. Who are the partners that have a role to play in doing better?	5. Who are the partners that have a role to play in doing better?
6. What works to do better, including no-cost and low-cost ideas?	6. What works to do better, including no cost and low-cost ideas?
7. What do we propose to do?	7. What do we propose to do?

Although the questions seem identical, they are crafted to stimulate change in two similar, but separate environments. The population questions will identify steps that will shape your program's contribution to improving quality of life. The performance questions will organize actions to improve the quality of your program's service delivery.

Answers to the population and performance questions, will form the cornerstone of your strategy to achieve Measurable Impact. They provide a foundation for analyzing our challenge. They make everyone feel invested in the strategy because people enjoy being asked for their input. Finally, they ensure that you have all the right people at the table to begin with. If the team or organization can't answer these questions, it must be expanded it to include the people that can. Hopefully, you already have the right people on your team. But you may have to make some substitutions along the way (we'll cover that in Chapter 4).

The population vs. performance distinction is what separates RBA from all other frameworks. Population accountability organizes our work with co-equal partners to promote community well-being. Performance accountability organizes our work to have the greatest impact on our customers. What we do for our customers is our contribution to community impact. At both the population and performance accountability levels, the "compass" pointing to the grail of Measurable Impact shows the series of steps and strategies taken by individual and organizational partners.

But remember, no matter how quickly your team buys into the goal of Measurable Impact, they still need you to lead them to it. It's the key to this whole quest (that's why it's in the title of the book). As the captain of the ship, you need to model the behavior you wish to see in others. Through your leadership, your team will learn not only what you aim to achieve, but how you aim to do it, and why it matters. Your motivation will help drive their commitment. Your focus will keep them working smarter, not harder. Your integrity will set the guidelines for what is and is not acceptable.

As you'll see in Chapters 3 and 4, leadership is critical to changing the culture of a community and the culture of an organization. At both the population and performance level, leadership helps put others on the path to achieving measurable results. This takes time and you need to manage it every step of the journey. Culture change is scary—there will be resistance—and the only way to overcome this is to provide inspiration and persistence.

Finding the Grail by Creating a Culture of Results in Your Community

What is a community?

- California is the most populous state in the U.S. with over 37 million people. It encompasses fifty-eight counties and 482 incorporated cities and towns. It was once one of the most linguistically diverse areas in the U.S, with seventy indigenous languages derived from native Indian tribes.

- Central Iowa is composed of the three counties surrounding Des Moines, Iowa. Roughly 570,000 people live in the region. Eighty-nine percent of the residents graduate from high school and the average income is $62,000. Twenty-two percent of the population is living in poverty.

- Nashville is the capital of the Tennessee, home to the Grand Ole Opry and the Country Music Hall of Fame, known to the world as "Music City." The city enjoys sprawling farmland, a bustling downtown area, and a regional commercial hub. It is 60% White, 27% African American, 8.4% Hispanic, and 3.1% Asian.

- Eastside Neighborhood, San Antonio, Texas: The Eastside Neighborhood of downtown San Antonio spans less than four square miles and has a strong Hispanic population. Roughly sixty percent of young people live in poverty and an equal proportion of adults do not have a high school diploma, according the 2005-2009 American Community Survey.

Each of these examples gives a sense of community. Webster's provides three similar definitions of community:

1. a unified body of individuals;
2. a body of persons or nations having a common history or common social, economic, and political interests; and
3. a people with common interests living in a particular area.

But defining community in terms of "common" characteristics doesn't get us very far. We need to drill deeper. Communities are about more than just what people *share,* they're about how people *relate.* The relationships formed between people who live in the same town, work in the same profession, or believe in the same mission are the cornerstones of those communities. And it is the *strength* of those relationships which determines whether a community will succeed at achieving its desired results and creating Measurable Impact.

To take that point one step further, we don't necessarily even have to know what a community's goals are in order to determine whether it will succeed. Whether it aims to ensure that its children succeed in school or promote a vibrant economy, a community with tight-knit, effective relationships among its members is more likely to meet its mark. The bonds formed in these communities are based on relationships that value individual and joint accountability—or to put it another way—communities which value a culture of results.

In these communities, people develop a habit of working together in support of varied purposes. That repeated interaction not only builds trust but also an understanding that their relationships come with a responsibility to at least try to collaborate effectively. These types of community members know their roles and also how their contributions will affect the whole. Where there is a culture of results, people form partnerships of real purpose and work towards achieving a specific goal, not just to raise their own publicity or meet their own private interests.

So, you want to change the culture of your community? Here are three ways to do it. You can:

1. move to a new community that has the culture you seek;

2. pester and annoy everyone that doesn't agree with you in your current community until they leave; or

3. inspire the people in your community to share your vision and work towards a common goal.

There are definitely times when options (1) and (2) seem like the best—and even the easiest—choice. But we know better. As I said in Chapter 2, moving your community towards real, tangible, life-affirming change takes a lot of work. The only real option on the table is (3) (if it were anything else, this would be a much shorter book).

Creating a culture of results requires: leadership, better funding decisions, and effective communication.

Leadership: Key Leaders are Key

The most important requirement for changing cultures and achieving Measurable Impact is leadership. As custodians of a community's values, leaders can inspire stakeholders and mobilize them to do more than they could do individually. Additionally, they can help their peers prioritize achieving results for the community over their own self-interest.

Leaders come in all shapes and sizes and from all sectors. Some are managers of non-profits, directors of government agencies, business executives, and elected officials. No matter what their title, though, they can set the direction for improving conditions of well-being for the children and families of their community. And great leaders affirm the culture of results by holding themselves accountable for demonstrating Measurable Impact.

We also know that without strong leaders, communities suffer. Consider this (see Exhibit B):

In 1999, a select group of Maryland legislators, supported with funding from the Annie E. Casey Foundation, took up a self-imposed challenge: how do we improve the quality of life for the greatest number of Maryland's children?

Their initiative led to the creation of the Joint Committee for Children, Youth and Families as a way for legislators in the Maryland General Assembly to focus on Measurable Impact. They carried the momentum forward into designing eight priority results and twenty-five indicators to gauge the State's progress.Involved with the committee were two legislative stars: up-and-comer Mark Shriver from the Maryland House of Delegates and the powerful State Senate Budget and Taxation committee Chair, Barbara Hoffman. In the wings, notable leaders like Delegate Paul Carlson were also ready to pick up the mantle.

Immediately, the Joint Committee selected "Children Entering School Ready to Learn" as the result upon which to develop a prototype. The Joint Committee's development of a prototype culminated in February 2001 with a Joint Budget Hearing on School Readiness held by the Senate Budget and Tax Committee and two House of Delegates Appropriations Committees.

This process led the way for new funding to be brought into the fold and old funding streams to be reallocated in more effective ways. Actions and strategies were implemented that have led to increase in children entering school ready to learn from 49 percent in 2001 to 81 percent in 2012. It seemed like there would be a clear path for the rest of the indicators to follow with the direction of the key leaders noted above.

But all of that changed in one election cycle.

Within less than three years, Mark Shriver left his seat to run for Congress, Barbara Hoffman lost her seat in the Senate, and Paul Carlson decided not to run. As a result, three of Maryland's most promising and powerful legislative leaders were no longer in play.

Unfortunately, this also meant that progress from the legislature stalled as well. While the results and indicators are still a cornerstone of the Governor's agenda for the Office for Children, the energy faded. The Joint Committee shifted focus away from the results and indicators, and there never was another Joint Budget hearing. And, subject to interpretation, the promise of Measurable Impact for Maryland's children has been left largely unfulfilled.

The story not only underscores the importance of leaders, it also illustrates the importance of *cultivating a pipeline of new leaders*. There are 188 members of the Maryland House of Delegates and State Senate. Shriver and Hoffman weren't the only legislators interested in children's well-being, but they did have significant "juice" and ability to make things happen. Both the State's children and its legislature would have benefited from a deeper bench, a stronger farm team, or a broader network of vocal child advocates involved in this initiative.

Going hand-in-hand with the need to cultivate leaders in your organization is the need to do so across multiple organizations. The legislative branch can't be as effective without leadership from the executive branch. The private sector needs strategic partners in the public sector. Think-tanks and academia count on entrepreneurs and politicians to put their ideas into action. Everyone in a leadership position should aim to draw support from partners working in parallel towards a shared vision. Developing these relationships expands the community and makes it easier to achieve a culture of results.

The chart on page 32 shows few examples of what works and what doesn't work for developing the leadership succession planning and pipeline development:

Exhibit B

THE PATH TO MEASURABLE IMPACT FOR CHILDREN IN MARYLAND AND WHERE THE TRAIL WENT COLD

Jan 1999	April 1999	Oct 1999	Oct 1999 - Jan 2000	April 2000	Jan 2001	Feb 2001	April 2001	2002 Election Cycle	2003- 2012
Eight results selected by the Maryland Partnership for Children and Youth	Maryland General Assembly creates Joint Committee on Children, Youth and Families	Joint Committee selects Children Entering School Ready to Learn to develop prototype for Results-Based Accountability	Joint Committee holds a seris of four public hearings with a coalition of stakeholders culminating in a framework for comprehensive strategy to improve school readiness in Maryland	2000 Maryland General Assembly approriates $10 million in FY2001 as initial funding for key elements to the strategy	Governor Glendening proposes $30 million in new funding for early care and education in his FY2002 budget	Senate and House of Delegates hold Joint Budget Hearing on School Readiness	2001 Maryland General Assembly appropriates $29.6 million in new funding for early childhood care and education in Maryland	Mark Shriver runs for Congress. Barbara Hoffman loses her re-election campaign after redistricting. Up and Comer Paul Carlson decides not to run for re-election	The percentage of chidren school ready to learn increases from 53% to 81% - See Appendix A. The 24 remaining indicators never went through the prototype process, including the Joint Budget Hearing, and their is no evidence in Measurable impact

THE PATH TO MEASURABLE IMPACT

TRAIL WENT COLD

Funding: Mo Money = Mo Problems

It should come as no surprise to anyone reading this book that the biggest challenge facing many in the social and non-profit sector is funding.

Those starting out can't do the work that has a positive impact on their community without money. But they can't get money without demonstrating the positive impact of their work.

More mature organizations often collaborate with like-minded partners in the front office but then have to compete with those same partners while drafting grant proposals, soliciting donors, and requesting budget allotments in the back office.

Faced with either a vicious cycle that seems impossible to break or the challenge to undercut others in your community doing great work, social sector organizations may think they have no good options when it comes to fundraising.

But consider this: if you ever find yourself choosing between two bad options, maybe you're asking yourself the wrong question.

Funding doesn't always need to be an "if-then" proposition. *If* we get this grant, then we will be able to expand recycling efforts. *If* our budget grows by 15 percent, then we will be able to expand access to education for

Works	Doesn't work
Identify key leaders to "own" the concept of Measurable Impact before and during your journey	Identify key leaders to "own" the concept of Measurable Impact after your journey starts or when its essentially over
As a key leader, be immediately thinking about what other key leaders can I get involved	As a key leader, make sure the effort is all about you and nobody else
Make sure the key leader attends critical meetings and participates	The key leaders sends his deputy or administrative assistant to take notes in his place

underrepresented minorities. *If* donors see the value in preventive medicine, then doctors will be able to counsel patients about the benefit of proper nutrition able to promote awareness about.

The reality is that as tight as budgets may seem, there is always another grant, another budget cycle, another donor. And although we all need money to carry on our work, leaders need to challenge the assumption that more money leads to greater impact. At your next brainstorming session about funding, start with this question:

If our community were starting from scratch in terms of the programs and strategies we fund, what would we do differently to achieve the results we want?

"The secret is to gang up on the problem, rather than each other."

Thomas Stallkamp

Community leaders should be prepared for an answer that may require changing the way they work. Why keep funding English as a Second Language (ESL) programs when a computer training program is the one that you need? Why bus students around the county to a remote after-school program, when a series of smaller, local programs have a greater impact with less of a burden on schools and families? By forcing your community to prioritize, you can cut out waste and focus on impact. You can stop doing things "just because" and start doing things "because they" *work*. And you can start to develop the low-cost and no-cost ideas that will support measurable results.

Leaders also need to challenge the assumption that fundraising is always a competitive, winner-take-all, game. If community partners share a vision, can complement each other's work, and help the same population, why not raise funds together? If anything, training funders and donors to focus on similar results using the same indicator data will lead to stronger and better funded programs across the community. A compelling plan for achieving Measurable Impact is a magnet for money. Funders want to buy success.

One local United Way, a funder of non-profits in its community, recently adopted this line of thinking. They changed their grant allocation strategy to focus on community results and indicators that gauged the education, income equality, and health of the community.

As the United Way's Income Committee, made up of volunteers, met to decide which programs they would fund, they had a collective epiphany. Why continue funding the forty or so grantees who've applied every year for the past twenty years, as a matter of course? The data showed redundancy of service providers. And when the Committee began asking tough questions, they realized that of those forty or so applications, they only needed to fund four if they were really serious about moving the needle on the indicator they cared about. These four programs were able to reach the same target population, provide the same services, at substantially less cost. And although the remaining thirty-six weren't immediately put on the chopping block, the United Way incrementally stopped funding underperforming and isolated programs in order to reward top performers that made the most difference in their communities.

Effective Communication: See Evil, Hear Evil, Speak Evil

Imagine that you came home from work to find your house on fire. Your neighbor walks over and tells you he saw the whole thing happen. But he didn't pick up a fire extinguisher, contact you, or call the fire department. How would you feel? Angry? Frustrated? Disappointed?

In communities all across the country the phenomenon of people seeing problems and doing nothing about them plays out day after day. There are fires going on throughout our community—in our neighborhoods plagued by violence, in our schools struggling to train our children, in the generations of families living on the outskirts of opportunity.

But if the community is not aware of the crisis, it can't be expected to solve it. That's why it's important for leaders to talk about these challenges openly and consistently. You may often have to alert the community to the problem. But even if the problem is widely recognized, folks may know the *effect* of the problem, but have no reliable information about the *cause of the problem.*

Consider the example of Strive, a Cincinnati-based coalition of non-profits, businesses, educators, and child advocates working to improve the lives of children. Their common belief was that education is the most important factor in giving children and families a way to escape the bondage of poverty. But there was also a common understanding that schools were struggling to seize that opportunity.

Everyone knew something was wrong. Parents saw it in falling test scores. Teachers saw it in the lowest ever graduation rates. Employers saw it in the growing number of students unprepared for college and the workforce. But what they couldn't see was a solution. Although there was plenty of data showing the *effect* of poor schools, there was almost no data showing the *cause* of poor schools.

The Strive coalition understood that they didn't necessarily need *more* data, they needed *better* data. And they needed the story behind the data. So they began engaging different stakeholders, sharing experiences, asking the tough questions, and generating one of the most extensive research efforts across Cincinnati's educational continuum. And after they collected all this information, they made it publicly available for all the child advocates, superintendents, civic associations, and business leaders to see.

That information prompted an informed, community-wide discussion about what was and wasn't working in the school system. Once they started asking the right questions, they got the right answers and made the right decisions. As a result, over the past four years, Cincinnati has made the greatest gains of any urban district on Ohio's school performance index. It has had the most success in shrinking the number of underperforming students and has demonstrated measurable progress on forty children's education indicators!

"The purpose of life is to collaborate for a common cause; the problem is nobody seems to know what it is."

Gerhard Gschwandtner

The Strive example highlights the importance of providing the community with reliable, trustworthy data about its challenges, and using indicator data that helps people wrap their heads around a problem and understand the collective story behind the curve. It's based on the premise that the more people you engage, the wider range of unique and unexpected gifts you'll be able to use to solve problems.

And it's our good fortune that we're in the midst of a growing movement to make more information public and transparent. Organizations like the Community Indicators Consortium and the National Neighborhood Indicators Partnership aim to promote the use of indicator data to foster discussion and inform policymaking. Across the country, cities and communities are sharing data on everything from dental health to environmental sustainability. More recently, Promise Neighborhoods, a U.S. Department of Education-funded program which seeks to improve education results in distressed communities, began supporting communities that make a commitment to Measurable Impact across a set of defined results and indicators.

But as anyone who's reading this probably knows, just telling people there's a problem usually isn't enough. You have to ask them to be part of the solution. Former Speaker of the House Tip O'Neill would often tell listeners that in his first run for Congress, he crisscrossed the district campaigning in every neighborhood in the district but his own. After his narrow win, he learned that his own next-door neighbor hadn't voted for him. Surprised, he asked the elderly woman whom he'd known all his life why. She responded, "Because you never asked."

There's no shortage of passion to make a measurable difference in our country. We are a charitable and hardworking society. But if we don't ask our community to get involved in, they won't. Put another way, my dad, a big basketball aficionado, once told me, "if you don't shoot, you can't score."

The main reason we have to explicitly call for support is to overcome what economists and social scientists describe as the "free rider problem." The phrase refers to the phenomenon where the individual benefits from a common, public good but avoids paying his or her fair share. That individual decision not to contribute doesn't threaten the public good, but if everyone adopted a similar stance the public good would disappear. Common examples are the tax cheat who benefits from public roads, free schools, and national defense; the public radio listener who never contributes to the cost of keeping his favorite program on the air; or the apartment-dweller whose home is protected by a neighborhood watch but never offers to take a shift.

There's a pretty good argument that free riding is entirely rational and logical. By deriving a benefit without paying the cost, you're maximizing your self-interest and achieving the most desirable outcome. But that's not sustainable in the long term. Over time, your actions not only reduce others' incentives to trust (and share the benefit), but they increase the likelihood that others will also decide to act in their self-interest, undermine collective action, and weaken the public good in the process.

But by asking people to contribute to collective action, we (hopefully) reduce the number of free-riders in the community. As a leader, you need to help others understand that if they each give a little of their time, talent and treasure to community effort, they have a better chance of sustaining the public good far into the future. Your request must reflect both the opportunity and the responsibility community members share in the public welfare.

How do you do that, you ask? There's one lesson that every star marketer, fundraiser, and community organizer will tell you: convince each person that their participation will make a difference. No matter how pressing or urgent a crisis seems, most people will only take action if they believe their efforts will cause some positive change.

Nicholas Kristof explains the phenomenon best in his 2009 article, *How to Save the World*. In it he describes a social psychology experiment in which participants are presented with an opportunity to support a compelling humanitarian cause. One group was asked to donate to fight widespread hunger ravaging the people of Mali. They received detailed descriptions about the scale of the problem complete with statistics and background information about the many hungry children in the country.

The second group was only asked to donate to help a single child from Mali, named Rokia, escape poverty. The results showed that people were far more willing to donate when they believed they had the ability to save a single person than when they were presented with a seemingly insurmountable crisis. As Kristof, summarizes "Donors didn't want to help ease a crisis personified by a child; they just wanted to help one person -and to hell with the crisis" Similarly, Mother Teresa once said, "If I look at the mass, I will never act. If I look at the one, I will."

The lesson for community leaders here is to communicate the impact on the individual, not just the group. The best way to draw more allies on your quest for Measurable Impact, is to highlight the role that each person can play in changing someone's life for the better. Because it's only in the context of the discrete, tangible work that individuals do each day, can we appreciate how the aggregation of all those hours served can have an impact we could never reach on our own. By creating a community plan that focuses on Measurable Impact, funders are also more likely to see and understand their role.

Aligning Your Organization towards the Grail

As a leader, the goals you set for your organization will be instrumental in achieving the change you want in your community. Consider the after-school program that triples the number of children who earn a B-plus or above; the Fire Department that can raise percentage of fires contained to the room of origin within a calendar year; or the foundation which meets its goal of ensuring that 75 percent of grantees make measurable improvements on their performance measures.

It doesn't matter what sector or field you're in. If you want to create a culture of results within your organization, make sure that those around you understand who the customer is and what they can do for him. Then create performance measures that will indicate whether the customer will be any better off from your service.

In order to improve the performance of your organization and simultaneously meet the needs of your community, you're going to need the right team. A strong organization should magnify the principles that guide your relationship with the community. It should be flexible, able to adapt to new circumstances, and learn from old mistakes. Above all, it should be the vehicle that enables you to align the performance of all relevant stakeholders to achieve Measurable Impact in your community.

Here are a few additional tips for aligning and improving the performance of your organization:

Tip 1. You Gotta Set the Table Before You Eat

Who are the most important people in your organization for you to support and focus your energies?

Most leaders would suggest that the hardest-working, most talented, or most passionate are the ones who carry the day. It's almost intuitive, that those who bring the most to your organization's mission would have the most impact.

But that's not always true. The people in your organization who should be highest on your radar might be the ones who are draining on your resources. The tension, stress, and extra work that result from your problem colleagues will prevent the organization from reaching its goals. That's not to say that the least talented and most resistant are deliberately sabotaging your operation. They're just making it a lot harder for everyone else to succeed.

> *"Once you have a staff of prepared, intelligent, and energetic people, the next step is to motivate them to be creative."*
>
> *Akio Morita*

The trick is to get rid of the dead wood quickly, while spending the majority of your time working with your most talented and most passionate colleagues. Make it clear to the resistant and problem colleagues that if they want to stick around, they will have to fall in line. Those who don't really care about conforming to a new way of business will make their way to the door. As Jim Collins points out in *Good to Great*, one of the most important things great leaders can do is make sure they have the right people on the bus. Conversely, the wrong people need to get off the bus.

Think of this as a real-life application of the 80/20 rule (also known as the Pareto principle). Simply stated, 80 percent of the results come from 20 percent of the work. Another way to look at it is that the most talented 20 percent of your organization's workforce, produces 80 percent of your success. So if you want to get more bang for your buck, get rid of the folks holding you back so you can focus on the high performers.

Collaboration: an unnatural act by non-consenting adults.

unknown

This advice is echoed by experts in leadership as well. Doug Krug, co-author of the best-selling book, *Enlightened Leadership,* tells those who attend his workshops that, "Where and how individuals and organizations focus their attention and energy dramatically impacts the results they achieve. You get more of what you focus on."

Similar to focusing on the right people, it is also important to focus on the right performance measures. When the Bureau for Primary Health Care (BPHC), the largest bureau in the Health Resources Services Administration, decided to improve performance of the 8,100 community health centers they fund to the tune of $6 billion, they chose a new set of eleven clinical performance measures as their way of tracking the return on investment.

Then, they changed the duties of their program officers from being just about ensuring paperwork compliance to facilitating performance improvement across 8,100 grantees nationwide. This was a paradigm shift for most employees. The Bureau also invested in new tools that not only helped community health centers collect and report the data, but also helped the program officers forge stronger relationships with the centers that led to meaningful conversations about how to improve the data. For nearly all of those program officers, that meant more writing, more visits, and more conference calls - certainly more effort. Those unwilling to adapt to the new process left. But the top performers were rewarded with recognition, and the culture began to slowly change.

The BPHC example goes to show what your organization can achieve if it "sets the table for success" by picking the right performance measures, collecting the right data and keeping the right people on the bus. Developing that awareness and skill takes practice, but once you have the data and the infrastructure, the rest is just figuring out the best way to use it and make it part of your culture.

Tip 2. Invest in yourself and others.

A shared belief among those working in the social sector is that education can unlock an individual's potential. Any investment that can develop one's social, economic, and professional development is worth the expense. There's even a bumper sticker that professes, "If you think education is expensive, try ignorance."

In our case, what's true for individuals is also true for organizations. Investing in the development of your team is almost always worth the cost. If you're a manager, take an interest in your staff's training and education. You (or someone) else presumably hired them because they brought certain skills or experiences to the job, right? So take the opportunity to develop those skills and improve the quality of your organization's work.

With online and e-Learning courses flourishing, it's now easier than ever for your team to build their skillsets without leaving the job. Take the lead in finding out what classes, workshops or training sessions would be most applicable to your field. If you can, subsidize these programs or set aside time each month or year for continuing education.

Note that training need not always come from formal education. Conferences, networking events, lecture series, and even brown bag lunches can provide great opportunities to learn and grow as a professional. Encourage everyone in your organization to attend at least two of these events a year.

Of course, not all of these events are free. And for managers of organizations with tight budgets, many of them may worry, "What if I train my staff and they leave?" But the more daunting question is, "What if you *don't* train them and they *don't* leave? That possibility certainly won't bring you Measurable Impact.

Tip 3. Practice makes perfect

Transforming your organization will take time. Even if you adopt the RBA framework and its tools, change still won't happen overnight. It will take time for leadership to understand the methodology, implement it, and get feedback from the rest of the organization. But that's OK, because every day you and your team work at it, you'll get better.

I have two young boys whom I want to be star basketball players. A neighbor once noted, "The most important thing in training young athletes is 'time on the ball.'" Similarly, leaders need time practicing and using their tools to gain mastery at them. Along the way, you will no doubt make mistakes. Learn from them.

"You are what you repeatedly do.
Excellence is not an event -
it is a habit."

Aristotle

When learning how to apply RBA and make better use of data, don't be afraid to ask for help. Consider getting feedback from an expert consultant or start a practitioner's network - either within your organization or across partner organizations which share your mission. Like any other skill, there's only so much you can teach yourself. To master the craft, you may need to learn from those with more experience.

"The strength of the team is each individual member. The strength of each member is the team."

Phil Jackson

The leadership of a small non-profit organization in Washington, DC decided that the organization was moving in the wrong direction. The quality of the work had plummeted and the staff were not accountable for their commitments. So they decided to begin the RBA journey by investing in the capacity of their senior managers to use data to manage their respective departments. They received intensive group and one-on-one training, as well as expert coaching.

By then they were hooked, and outside consultant support was not enough for them. They wanted to create the structures needed to reinforce the concepts and create a new culture. They eventually began a "Measure of the Month" at their monthly executive team meetings, where each of the five managers rotated in presenting action plans for one of their respective performance measures. Not only did these sessions make the managers more focused, particularly when presenting to their peers and boss, but it also allowed each to get feedback and new ideas from the rest of management. The transparency in data, clarity of analysis, and execution of the subsequent action plan allowed the entire management team to engage in meaningful conversations that were never possible before. The managers then started to replicate this process within each department, and the performance of the organization shot through the roof. More funds were raised, more people received quality affordable housing and more residents found the supports they needed to get jobs and improve their health.

Tip 4. Don't market your tools. Market the impact of your work.

Although reference is made in this book to the value of RBA in achieving Measurable Impact, RBA is not an end in itself. It is a means through which you develop capacity to become effective. Rather than adding to your workload, it reframes the work you're already doing. As some would say, it's about working smarter, not harder.

It's easy to make the mistake of marketing the use of RBA or some other framework. But remember, this whole exercise—this whole quest—is for Measurable Impact. At the end of the day, the people you're helping and serving don't really care about the tools you used. They care about results you've achieved. Market your successes by demonstrating your own measurable improvements. If you have to market RBA, explain how better tools and better processes will generate better results for your organization's clients.

"Coming together is a beginning, staying together is progress, and working together is success."

Henry Ford

Consider the lesson learned by a state government program manager in Connecticut we'll call Larry. After a day-long training, Larry returned to his office excited and eager about what he'd just learned. He managed to mention RBA in every other sentence, regardless of the topic. Listening to Larry, you would think RBA alone would feed the hungry, cure the sick, and even raise the dead. And although Larry did a great job of describing what RBA could empower practitioners to do, he did a lousy job of explaining what RBA would do to help his team succeed at their jobs. It didn't take long for Larry to become the guy everyone was talking *about* but no one wanted to talk *to*. And so instead of encouraging his team to adopt the framework, Larry ended up annoying (and alienating) the people he wanted to engage.

Instead, Larry should have rallied his team behind the Measurable Impact they wanted to achieve. If he had been focused on whatever performance measure that his team cared about m, he would have been better able to tap into the passion of his colleagues. By using RBA ideas such as asking the either set of the Seven Questions of Accountability on a regular basis (without calling it RBA), they probably would also have been less resistant.

Tip 5. Celebrate success.

Nothing motivates people more than public recognition (except maybe free food). Even the humblest among us appreciates being recognized for his efforts. That's why kids who get straight A's in elementary school sit at the front of the classroom. That's why we created award ceremonies. That's why many people, for better or worse, decide to run for public office.

You can tap into this phenomenon to inspire those around you to succeed. For some, being celebrated for a job well done can be even more rewarding than monetary compensation. That sense of validation, especially among one's peers, is impossible to put a price on.

Another reason why leaders should recognize positive accomplishments is that it's the best way to reinforce the type of work you want others to produce. Watching others lauded changes the way we think about our own efforts and goals. We start saying to ourselves, "If Bob, Debbie, and Steve can be Employee of the Month, then what's stopping me?"

Celebrating success in our organizations not only generates positive energy, it also helps build momentum. Knowing that we've improved a performance measure, reached a milestone, or broken a record suggests that we're headed in the right direction_that we're on the path to more good news in the future. And if at times, those wins seem few and far between, recognizing them when they occur can relieve anxiety about meeting the next goal down the line.

5

The Personal Challenge: Will You Be Ready for the Grail?

You've been on your journey for a while now, and the Holy Grail is almost within sight. Let's stop and take stock of how far you've come.

With the tools and tips at your disposal, you've clearly defined success for both your community and organization. You're focused, organized, and determined to seize the day.

You know what it will take to engage your community. You can work with civic associations, business leaders, government officials and other stakeholders in charting a path to progress. And the others in your organization share your passion and your vision for Measurable Impact. So what's left?

This is a question only you can answer. The lessons you've learned in this book will get you as far as you want them to take you. But you have to decide how much energy you're willing to put in and how much comfort you're willing to give up.

Governments and non-profits will spend billions of dollars each year on leadership development programs. But all of that is wasted, if leaders lack an understanding of the Measurable Impact that the money is intended to support.

Simply stated, no amount of training can give a leader his or her *purpose.*

There is no point of spending thousands of dollars on leadership development training, if we don't know what impact we want to achieve. That's why Measurable Impact, for customers and communities, starts with individuals first making a measurable change in their own behavior, and public leaders need to know they are becoming better leaders in the service of results and Measurable Impact.

You may want to expand your ability to collaborate with school board colleagues at an individual level, increase the percentage of children able to read proficiently at the program level, and raise high-school graduation rates at the community level. Identify your purpose first and let it guide your actions. That should be the cornerstone of any individual leadership development efforts.

Only with this type of deliberate and unrelenting focus on individual, organizational and community behavior will you see change. And with that change comes Measurable Impact.

"Teamwork is the ability to work together toward a common vision. The ability to direct individual accomplishments toward organizational objectives. It is the fuel that allows common people to attain uncommon results."

Andrew Carnegie (1835 - 1919)
American industrialist

That's why this book is framed by the story of the Holy Grail. The hero, on the verge of attaining the chalice, must be ready to bear the burden. Even though the Grail will be different for each individual, like Percival or Galahad, legendary medieval grail-seekers that had proven themselves worthy when presented with the grail, leaders in the midst of achieving Measurable Impact must prepare themselves accordingly.

"Gettin' good players is easy. Gettin' 'em to play together is the hard part."

Casey Stengel (1890 - 1975)
American baseball player and manager

That kind of preparation can't be taught. It comes from within. It is born of purpose. It springs from the character, integrity, and commitment common to all those willing to share the desire to serve. Leadership has to be more than a desire to be in the limelight. It's about realizing that there will always be people who can be guided by the light of your example.

The Holy Grail of Public Leadership is out there and it can be found. The only question is: will you be the one to attain it?

Appendix A:

Examples of
Measurable Impact

Population Examples:

1. State of Maryland: Percentage of Children Entering School Ready to Learn. - pg. 62

2. Santa Cruz County, California: Percentage of 11th Graders Reporting Drinking Alcohol in the Last 30 Days. - pg. 64

3. Newcastle Upon Tyne, United Kingdom: Percentage of 16-19 year olds Not in Education, Employment or Training (NEET). - pg. 68

Performance Examples:

1. Penrith (Australia): Better Early Childhood Outcomes Project: Percentage of Early Childhood Professionals with Increased Knowledge About the Different Ways Agencies Can Work Together. - pg. 70

2. Baltimore City Department of Social Services: Number of Children in Out of Home Care. - pg. 72

3. Epilepsy Unit (Cardiff, Wales): Average Waiting Time to See a Specialist. - pg. 74

Population Examples

Population Example 1:
Percentage of Children Entering School Ready to Learn.

Location: State of Maryland

Author: Rolf Grafwallner, Assistant State Superintendent, Division of Early Childhood Development, Maryland State Department of Education.

Result: Children Enter School Fully Ready to Learn

Indicator: Percentage of children entering kindergarten fully ready to learn.

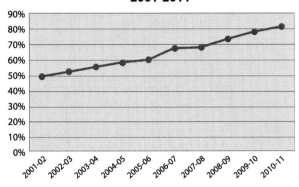

Figure A
A PERCENTAGE OF CHILDREN ENTERING KINDERGARTEN FULLY READY TO LEARN 2001-2011

What happened?

The positive results in recent years are not due to any single strategy, but a combination of the following methods to boost school readiness skills for young children:

- Taking a strategic approach to aligning early childhood education and K-12 education reforms.

- Linking child outcomes to improvements in the early care and education system (e.g., establishing program improvement, workforce development, and standards-based early learning).

- Addressing the readiness gaps for subgroups of children and generating momentum to improve learning opportunities for those children.

What was the biggest leadership challenge?

The establishment of a Kindergarten Entry Assessment (KEA) as the basis for RBA performance measures was a new concept for all constituency groups, including policymakers, local school systems and early childhood community. The challenge lay in educating the constituencies that the use of the data, being used within the context of RBA, fosters program improvement, and is not the basis for a high-stakes accountability system.

What were the key lessons learned?

The use of the KEA data as part of the RBA process has transformed the policies, operations, and business practices for the early childhood community across the state. The annual results are now being used by the legislature, executive branch, local school systems, and county governments. The RBA process has been implemented by MSDE's Division of Early Childhood Development as part of the grants management process for statewide networks of services, including the Judy Center Partnership, family support centers, child care resource and referral agencies.

Population Example 2:
Percentage of 11th Graders Reporting Drinking Alcohol in the Last 30 Days.

Location: Santa Cruz County, California.

Authors: Susan Brutschy and Deanna Zachary.

Result: Youth make good decisions.

Indicators: Percentage of youth using alcohol in the last 30 days.

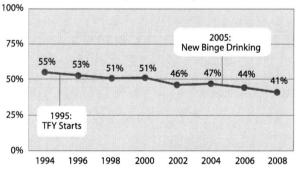

Figure B
PERCENTAGE OF SANTA CRUZ COUNTY 11th GRADERS REPORTING ALCOHOL USE IN THE LAST 30 DAYS (1994 - 2008)

Source: The American Drug and Alcohol Survey, 1994-1998.
California Healthy Kids Survey, 2000-2009

What happened?

Santa Cruz County, California had especially high rates of teen drug and alcohol abuse, including binge drinking (defined as five drinks for men and four drinks for women in about two hours), as shown in the first community assessment in Santa Cruz County, in 1995. The numbers shocked the community and prompted a coalition of 110 organizations known as Together for Youth/Unidos Para Nuestros Jovenes (TFY/UPNJ) to form with the support of United Way of Santa Cruz County. TFY/UPNJ developed five desired outcomes and seven strategies to decrease youth alcohol and drug use. Meanwhile, a "What Works" Steering Committee was also created in the county and served as an RBA- "think tank", providing guidance to many different change efforts, especially TFY/UPNJ. From 1994-2006, alcohol use decreased from 55 percent to 44 percent of 11th graders . However, the high rate of youth binge drinking in the county persisted remaining much higher than comparable figures for state overall.

TFY/UPNJ decided to focus their efforts on youth binge drinking and they used RBA in their environmental prevention strategies to raise community awareness, limit youth access to alcohol, and increase the legal consequences of providing alcohol to youth for retailers and parents. Youth ages 16 to 20 from all different backgrounds were surveyed by other youth about their binge drinking behavior, and over time, binge drinking fell from 66 percent of youth in 2006 to 59 percent in 2007, after the interventions.

What was the biggest leadership challenge?

The TFY/UPNJ project had buy-in from many local law enforcement agencies, but not all. Santa Cruz County has a long history of tolerance for providing alcohol to youth, and a high tolerance for marijuana use among residents. The coalition needed to better educate some law enforcement personnel about the dangers of binge drinking for youth and the importance of environmental prevention efforts. Also, many parents and community members were unaware about the dangers of binge drinking for youth including drinking and driving, alcohol poisoning, unplanned or unwanted sexual activity, and violent behavior.

What were the key lessons learned?

The early years of TFY/UPNJ were dedicated to the larger issue of youth drug and alcohol use, and after the effort achieved some success, more work was needed to turn to the emerging issue of binge drinking, and to create new partnerships and strategies. One of the key features of RBA is how it includes a wide range of stakeholders using different methods to improve outcomes. In the case of TFY/UPNJ, there were multiple efforts that were necessary for success, and strategies needed to change over time including: a grand jury report; leadership training for youth; community-wide public education; education of law enforcement personnel and parents; new alcohol laws including social host ordinances in multiple cities; decreasing sales to minors; increasing community knowledge of the consequences of binge drinking; and an awards program for responsible alcohol merchants. That flexibility made it possible to make the best us of all our tools, in collaboration, to deliver lower alcohol abuse rates.

The best executive is the one who has sense enough to pick good men to do what he wants done, and self-restraint to keep from meddling with them while they do it.

Theodore Roosevelt

Population Example 3:
Percentage of 16-19 year olds Not in Education, Employment or Training (NEET)

Location: Newcastle Upon Tyne, United Kingdom.

Author: Sara Morgan-Evans, formerly Connexions Manager and Head of Integrated Youth Services for Newcastle upon Tyne.

Result: A greater percentage of 16-19 year olds in Newcastle upon Tyne accessing education, employment and training post 16 and therefore more likely to go on to Achieve Economic Well-Being in adult life.

Indicator: Percentage of 16-19 year olds not in education, employment or training (NEET).

What happened?

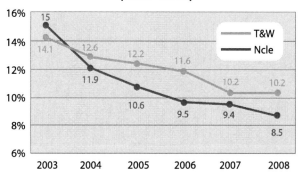

Figure C
**PERCENTAGE OF 16-19 YEAR OLDS
NOT IN EDUCATION OR TRAINING (NEET)
(2003 - 2008)**

Sara Morgan-Evans attended training for RBA and also trained as a trainer. She disseminated the methodology to the full staff team and asked them to adopt it as their way of working with individual clients, their full caseload of young people, and partners supporting positive outcomes for young people. The team realized that by using the RBA approach for individuals they would more easily trigger positive results across the population of clients that they serve for the group of.

What was the biggest leadership challenge?

Initially, convincing team members that the RBA method would really have an impact posed the greatest challenge. However, by encouraging them to write up case studies and by disseminate the falling NEET percentage on a weekly basis, they were able to see both their individual and the collective team impact which helped to keep morale high. Eventually even the skeptical were convinced that by adopting the RBA approach they could make a measurable difference in their work.

What were the key lessons learned?

The most important lesson learned was to ensure that the whole team is involved in using RBA in their work - even that receptionists-because they are the first people a client encounters and can make or break the client's experience.

The team also recognized the value in positive encouragement and giving due credit for contributing to the achievement of targets. We found that keeping the charts showing progress on the wall kept the team updated regularly. And the discovery that complacency will always set you back, served to focus our attention and inspire our best work.

Performance Examples

Performance Example 1:
Number of Children in Out of Home Care

Location: Penrith, NSW Australia.

Author: Louisa McKay, Service Capacity Building Project Manager, Family Services, New South Wales.

Program: Better Early Childhood Outcomes..

Performance Measure: Percentage of Early Childhood Professionals with Increased Knowledge about the Different Ways Agencies Can Work together.

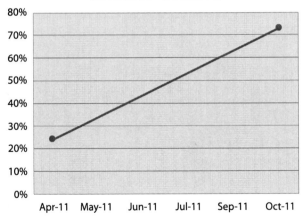

Figure D
PERCENTAGE OF EARLY CHILDHOOD PROFESSIONALS WITH INCREASED KNOWLDGE ABOUT THE DIFFERENT WAYS AGENCIES CAN WORK (APR. 2011 - OCT. 2011)

What happened?

Performance measures were clearly defined and measured prior to the commencement of any deliverables.

Once the data was formalized we commenced three forums that provided opportunities for networking, consultation, generation of ideas and feedback from early childhood and family support professionals. We inquired about out their ideas, how they were collaborating other agencies, and how they felt they might improve.

Based on the feedback and analysis we developed an action plan that included the provision of training sessions, working groups, and an online screener to support referrals.

What was the biggest leadership challenge?

This project was rolled out in collaboration with a local council and overall the partnership worked well. However, waiting for certain responses before moving on to the next action could sometimes be a challenge. Otherwise, this project ran smoothly with efficient meetings, clear measures, purpose and actions.

What were the key lessons learned?

Start with the data you have-at the population and program level. We used online survey tools like Survey Monkey, which was useful and easy way to collect data from other agencies and partners. But you only need one data point to get started, don't postpone the analysis until you're overwhelmed by data

From that point on include as many professionals in the process and provide feedback on a regular basis. Sometimes that feedback should be provided one on one, but often collective feedback in the form of meetings and public forums are critical. Focus on sharing ideas, gaining new knowledge, and the importance of your common goals.

Performance Example 2:
Number of Children in Out of Home Care Location: Baltimore, Maryland.

Author: Molly McGrath Tierney.

Program: Baltimore City Department of Social Services.

Performance Measure: Number of Children in Out of Home Care.

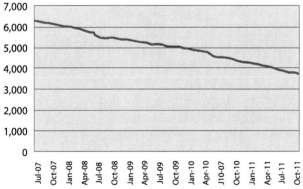

Figure E
**NUMBER OF CHILDREN IN OUT OF HOME CARE
(Jul. 2007 - Oct. 2011)**

What happened?

By mid 2007, the number of children in foster care in Baltimore City had ballooned to three times the national average. We began by articulating a simple mission: we believe children should be in families and in permanent families as quickly as possible. This was quickly follows by the rigorous use of child specific data for decision making and a business practice that ensures priority tasks are successfully completed. In short, each time a task is identified (adoptions) we broke it down into "component parts" (here are the specifically named children on *your* caseload eligible for adoption), applied to it a "structured activity" (here are the specific tasks, in order, that have to be done to complete an adoption) and assigned to it a "deadline" (due by next Tuesday). This business practice - component parts, structured activities, and deadlines -has contributed heavily to our success.

What was the biggest leadership challenge?

Organizational culture nurtured a pattern of distant executives providing directives to front line staff and, when they failed, permitting the community to blame the worker. Little attention had been given to ensuring the worker's success. The biggest leadership challenge was developing a leadership team who would refrain from "do-as-I-say" use of authority and instead commit to the meticulous design of implementation plans on the front end. In doing so, we began to work backwards from the worker's success, and were more likely to prove our staff the tools and support they needed to do their jobs.

What were the key lessons learned?

Don't underestimate the scale of design implementation plans on the front end required to ensure the success of an urban child welfare agency.

Performance Example 3:
Average Waiting Time to See a Specialist

Location: Cardiff, Wales, United Kingdom.

Author: Ruth Jordan and Vicki Myson.

Program: Patients with a First Suspected Seizure or Unexplained Blackout in Cardiff and the Vale of Glamorgan.

Performance Measure(s): Percentage of patients Seen by a Specialist within the Two Week (NICE Guideline);

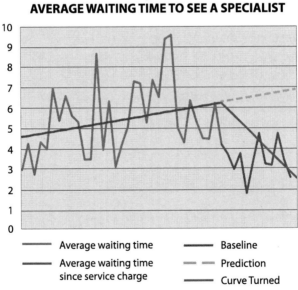

Figure H
AVERAGE WAITING TIME TO SEE A SPECIALIST

Average waiting time	Baseline
Average waiting time since service charge	Prediction
	Curve Turned

What Happened?

NICE Guidance for Epilepsy (CG20) recommends that patients experiencing a first suspected seizure should be seen by a specialist within two weeks to minimise the risk of harm and misdiagnosis. The epilepsy team used RBA to develop services for this patient group including a new epilepsy specialist nurse led emergency unit service, joint clinics and fast track access for general practitioners and education programmes for members of the multi-disciplinary team.

What was the biggest leadership challenge?

Data monitoring had previously been viewed negatively to identify and hold to account teams and individuals who were perceived to be under-performing. The biggest leadership challenge faced was empowering and inspiring members of the clinical team to positively view and respond to data in order to turn the curves.

What were the key lessons learned?

A full range of partner involvement from the beginning of the programme, in this case including patient representatives, can help to drive low cost service improvements that are both supported by and supportive of service users.

Appendix B:

Additional Resources

Additional Resources for Finding the Holy Grail

1. www.raguide.org, Results-Based Accountability™ Implementation Guide, Mark Friedman's website with How To Questions and Answers.

2. www.resultsaccountability.com, Mark Friedman's website with the latest in Results-Based Accountability™ news and information.

3. Friedman, Mark. *Trying Hard is Not Good Enough*. Trafford Publishing. 2005.

4. www.resultsleadership.org, Results Leadership Group website with information on consultants, trainers and facilitators that can support your quest. The following useful articles can also be found:

   a. Achieving Collective Impact with Results-Based Accountability™, by Deitre Epps

   b. ResultsStat Overview, by Lee, Luecking, Friedman and Boyd.

5. www.resultsscorecard.com: Results Scorecard is a web-based strategic management tool developed to support the Results-Based Accountability™ framework.

Do you want to create Measurable Impact? Take the 14 element self-assessment guide found at www.resultsleadership.org/self-assessment. A Result Leadership Group consultant will contact you to discuss the results.

Additional Readings on Accountability and Leadership:

1. Behn, Robert D. *Rethinking Democratic Accountability.* Brookings. 2001.

2. Fisher, Roger , and William Ury, *Getting to Yes* . Random House Business Books. 2003.

3. Heifetz, Ronald A., and Marty Linsky *Leadership on the Line: Staying Alive through the Dangers of Leading,* Harvard Business School Press. 2002.

4. Krug, Doug ,and Ed Oakley, *Enlightened Leadership: Getting to the Heart of Change* .Simon and Schuster Canada. 1994.

5. Pink, Daniel. *Drive: The Surprising Truth About What Motivates Us.* Riverhead Books. 2009

6. Schorr, Lisbeth B. *Common Purpose: Strengthening Families and Neighborhoods to Rebuild America.* Doubleday.1997.

7. Senge, Peter . *The Fifth Discipline: The Art and Practice of the Learning Organization.*Doubleday. 1990.

Appendix C:

Short Essay

The Four Public Leaders You Will Meet While Turning Curves

In community change efforts, the way leaders work with each other is an important collaborative exercise. The facilitation and engagement of leaders in the process is a critical aspect of whether the holy grail of public leadership is achieved - Measurable Impact.

The Results-Based Accountability™ framework, as described by Mark Friedman in the book, "Trying Hard is Not Good Enough" lays out a way for leaders to take collaborative action in a data-driven community change effort. In the framework, the notion of "Turning a Curve" is making a Measurable Impact for something important to your community or the customers your organization serves. To effectively facilitate turn the curve discussions or even get others to participate in turning curves, you need to understand how to inspire and work with different types of people.

From my experience and drawing heavily from the Temperament Types of the Myers-Briggs Type Indicator[2] as originally described by David Keirsey, there are four types of leaders who can help you turn a curve. The four leaders include Rule Followers, Thrill Seekers, Energizers, and Strategizers. They can be found among the world's population and can be an asset if approached strategically. To capitalize on these leaders not only will you need to manage your communication with them, but how they communicate with each other. Here is how you know them when you see them:

ENGAGING LEADERS TO HELP YOU TURN A CURVE[3]

	Rule Followers	Thrill Seekers	Energizers	Strategizers
What excites them most about implementing Results-Based Accountability™	The discipline and rigor of the Turn the Curve thinking process; using data	Getting from talk to action quickly; putting out a "community fire"	Saving the world; helping others reach full potential	Personal sense of accomplishment of turning a curve; achieving competence
You need to act this way for the leader to believe in you	Present information logically, sequentially, with relevant data available, treat them fairly	Be fun and spontaneous, give no judgment and freedom to act as they see fit	Give warmth, enthusiasm, humor, individual recognition, positive feedback	Treat them with respect, to respect your competence
To act in helping to turn a curve, a person of this type often:	Needs a practical reason, tests your awareness of facts and details	Needs to see the challenge and fun, and ability to fix the problem	Needs ability to imagine the possibilities and create with others	Needs clear goals and notes long-term aspects or trends

Rule Followers (41% of the population) are typically drawn to positions that include administrators, lawyers, contract managers, and finance people. Words often used to describe Rule Followers include overseer, supporter, examiner, and defender. They like order and have a high sense of duty, responsibility, and loyalty. They prefer step by step instructions and want others to see them as hard working, reliable, and dependable. Rule Followers can often slow down the turning of curves by being too bureaucratic. They can accelerate the turning of curves by helping the group be prepared with the information they need to make good decisions.

Thrill Seekers (33% of the population) are typically drawn to positions that include detectives, firefighters, litigators, and social workers. Words often used to describe Thrill Seekers include entertainer, craftsman, and artist. They hate meetings, particularly repetitive and unproductive meetings that don't facilitate mental stimulation. They are laid back, open minded, and love to live life. They need to be actively involved to meet their in the moment needs. They want others to see them as resourceful and risk taking and want to be known for their spontaneity. Thrill Seekers can often slow down the turning of curves by being too expedient and making quick decisions. They can use their quick wit and desire for change to positively accelerate the turning of curves by thinking outside of the box to bring new resources to the table.

Energizers (14% of the population) are typically drawn to positions that include trainers/teachers, coaches, counselors, and spokespeople. Words often used to describe Energizers include mentor, advocate, visionary, and dreamer. They seek harmony in the work place. Big ideas are at the forefront for Energizers and details or step-by-step directives tend to be of less importance. It defies their individuality. They can create a vision and easily motivate others to follow it. They want others to see them as authentic and inclusive and want to be known for their ability to inspire others. Energizers can often slow down the turning of curves by being too idealistic and by overlooking relevant details. The abilities of an Energizer can accelerate the turning of curves by inspiring others to take action and by their sheer passion.

Strategizers (12% of the population) are typically drawn to positions that include judges, computer programmers, scientists, and executives. Words often used to describe Strategizers include chief, intellectual, originator, and engineer. They can be a visionary and a builder of systems. They tend to be more impersonal and bring logic to ideas and actions. They want others to see them as competent and logical and above all want to be known for their expertise. Has the ability to strategically analyze complex issues. Strategizers can often slow down the turning of curves by being too competitive with others. They can accelerate the turning of curves by bringing all the right players to the table and do at all costs mentality.

Once you have identified the types of leaders you have around you, there are several ways to engage them to productively help you turn curves in your work. Approaches to navigating the characteristics of these four leadership types are outlined in the chart below.

Understanding what drives leadership behavior and how to use this knowledge to motivate behavior is the key to collaborative action. If leaders can't work together, they will never break from traditional stove-pipe behavior needed to attain the holy grail of solid Measurable Impact.

Appendix D:

Short Essay

The Drive for Public Leadership: Using Purpose, Mastery, and Autonomy to Create Measurable Impact

While recently reading the New York Times Bestselling book, *Drive*, by Daniel Pink, I realized that many of the concepts he talked about were variations of the same points that I was making in this book, *The Holy Grail of Public Leadership*. Importantly, he offered that individuals need to have purpose, mastery, and autonomy to have motivation needed to truly succeed in the workplace and in life. These same three elements are also needed to create a Measurable Impact.

Purpose in the sense that they need to understand how their work contributes to the greater good, mastery in that you want to improve every day and know whether or not you did and autonomy in that the ends (measurable impact) of your work are more important than the means (whether you showed up at 9am and left at 5pm or have control of your own hours).

Given the success of *The New York Times* bestseller *Drive* and over nine million views of the corresponding YouTube video a re-introduction of these three elements as a way of creating Measurable Impact by using concepts found in the Results-Based Accountability™ (RBA) framework as defined by Mark Friedman in the book, *Trying Hard is Not Good Enough*.

I. Purpose and Measurable Impact

The use of Results statements in the RBA framework are a declaration of purpose. They are conditions of well-being that everyone can agree on. They are the reason you get up in the morning and ultimately the purpose of the quest for Measurable Impact.

The idea of public leaders needing a clear sense of purpose is not a new one. In the book *Common Purpose* by Lee Schorr, Schorr argues that "a clear, long term mission"[4] is a critical ingredient to transforming whole inner city neighborhoods by reducing child abuse, school dropout rates, teenage pregnancy and juvenile crime. Traveling with Schorr in the early 90's while working for the Center for the Study of Social Policy, Mark Friedman was influenced by this idea when creating the RBA framework.

More recently, Kania and Kramer in the famed article "Collective Impact" in the Stanford Social Innovation Review, offer a "Common Agenda" as one of the five conditions of collective success. Their view is that achieving Measurable Impact "requires all participants to have a shared vision for change, one that includes a common understanding of the problem and a joint approach to solving it through agreed upon actions." They go further to state, "Every participant need not agree with every other participant on all dimensions of the problem. In fact, disagreements continue to divide participants in all of our examples of collective impact. All participants must agree, however, on the primary goals for the collective impact initiative as a whole."[5]

This shared vision, or "Common Agenda", among employees creates a dedication to the mission that is a greater motivator than any incentive, monetary or otherwise. To provide an employee with a purpose creates a solid foundation for dedication and passion in any result achieved. Without purpose the notion of Collective Impact or the accountability created by Measurable Impact in using the RBA framework, is just a pipe dream. Dedication is created by purpose in work for staff members and the understanding that they are not just a cog in a larger machine, but an integral part of an organization's success.

The overwhelming perception of satisfaction in work is linked to money. "Satisfaction depends not merely on having goals, but on having the right goals" according to Pink.[6] Money is not the motive for creating satisfaction and purpose in work. Purpose can only be achieved if staff are paid just enough for salary to not be an issue and to be competitive and fair in relation to others in the organization. When issues of fairness are erased it allows an employee to focus on their work and progress toward the larger mission.

II. Mastery and Measurable Impact

There is no better way to know if you are mastering your work than by making measurable improvements or

Measurable Impact. RBA gives you the tools needed to create mastery.

Don't you want to know if you are getting better day to day? You need data to do this - indicators at the community level and performance measures at the program level.

Just as we counsel grantmakers and funders to shift from compliance to engagement relationships, working with your staff to pick the right measures will set the right tone? In selecting performance measures, focus on better off measures instead of how much or how well measures.

Pink says that "mastery is the desire to get better and better at something that matters."[7] This mastery allows employees to define for themselves what matters. If the topic of an employee's mastery can be measured it provides the ability to actually create a Measurable Impact through their hard work and passion.

The driving force behind most public leaders is to create positive results. RBA has the capability to create a positive impact in the social issues that our public leaders with to affect. Establish environments where "the activity can be its own reward." That is why most of us went into public service. Because they were inspired by a noble cause and they wanted to make a difference. Somewhere along the way, this was forgotten. Having the right measures that they look at every day as the first thing they see in the morning and the last thing they see in the evening can be a powerful reminder to keep them inspired to continually improve.

Do something to challenge yourself to get better every day. That is why swimmers, swim and runners, run. Results-Based Accountability lays out the ends to help you find the means. These challenges can be turned into outcomes and drive progress if Measurable Impact can be seen using RBA. Progress keeps you on track toward your goals and helps you to see the fruits of your labor to improve mastery and future success. If you are mastering something, more likely than not your job will no longer feel like a job, but your pursuit of a passion.

Having the right measures will get you a long way but it isn't enough. People need quick feedback to know they are on the right track, which is why presenting data in trend lines gives people real time feedback on whether you are trending in the right direction. This allows for real time course corrections.

Mastery is a mindset that can't just be turned on or off by someone else. It has to be intrinsically motivated. Ever go to the gym because someone else told you to? No, you did it because you finally decided it was important.

Mastery takes time, but without a method of tracking progress and understanding of your work is not attainable. In the book Outliers Malcolm Gladwell argues that it takes 10,000 hours do become an expert[8], but if you are not consciously tracking your work it is not possible to understand how it impacts your progress.

No one will spend 10,000 hours of their life mastering a skill that they aren't passionate about. Sure, at first it may seem like a hassle to practice the piano every day for four hours, but if your love of music and learning are strong a mere interest eventually becomes a passion. Pink comes to this realization just as I do in my own book The Holy Grail of Public Leadership, "the joy is in the pursuit more than the realization."[9]

Pink writes that the three conditions of mastery are clear measures, immediate feedback, and challenges well matched to our abilities.[10] Connecting these conditions with the implementation of RBA helps to ensure that each step is achieved effectively.

III. Autonomy and Measurable Impact

The dedication created by the joy of the pursuit means that employees report to the mission. Working with a group whose sole purpose is to fill their role to create change and affect the mission creates a collective trust that allows for autonomy. The RBA focus on results makes you rigorous and leads to the autonomy needed for individuals to have the motivation to succeed.

In the nursing profession the number of patients seen during long shifts is more important that the individual patient outcome. Whether that means a missed critical detail when checking in a patient or just an overall degradation on bedside manner, this expectant quota changes the enjoyment and excitement of the profession for many nurses. The more hours worked means the more patients seen, but at what cost? Most nurses enjoy the ability to actually connect with patients and provide the attention that doctors are rarely able to provide due to demand. Being forced to quickly and mechanically tend to patients can drain the motivation and passion for the work and the job.

There is no quicker way to destroy the notion of autonomy, trust, and motivation than to set a quota. It takes the humanity out of the work especially when working in the public sector. Placing such a harsh lens on the outcome destroys the motivation to reach it. For Pink a profession like nursing would fall under "Motivation 3.0", "the link between how much time somebody spends and what that somebody produces is irregular and unpredictable."[11]

RBA encourages leaders to be tight on the "ends" and loose on the "means." If everyone can agree on the common purpose or results, then they should have the flexibility or autonomy to decide how to get there. Therefore, you need to trust your staff and community partners and give them discretion to make their own decisions.

Bob Behn, noted Harvard University professor agrees that staff autonomy is the key to impact in the book, Rethinking Democratic Accountability. The concept of accountability for results can often times be clouded by a focus on accountability for fairness and finances. To overcome this confusion on accountability focus requires discretion, which requires trust.[12] Trust allows autonomy for employees and creates a space that allows them to thrive and achieve outcomes.

Although RBA can help to create great outcomes, focusing on the wrong measure can setback progress. The wrong measure leads you to wrong results and unintended consequences, including unhappiness of staff. The evaluation of the public school teacher based on student test scores is currently an issue that argued from both sides. For decades the effectiveness of a teacher as ranked on their yearly evaluation has hinged on how well their students score on various standardized tests depending on the state. This focus on test scores is sometimes seen as the wrong measure because it means that a teachers across the classroom are teaching to the test instead of just focusing on teaching and instilling a love of learning in children to motivate them positively towards education. Perhaps the number we should evaluate teachers on should not be based on a standardized test but on the number of children that love learning.

More than setting your measures, it is important to be inflexible about making progress on the right measures. Be flexible about how your employees manage their time and resources together. Does it really matter if an employee is in the office from 9-5 everyday if they are the best at what they do at placing people after completion of the job training program? Do you really care if they took a long lunch or went to their kids school play in the middle of the day if they are a strong team member? Autonomy leads to mutual trust, between employee and manager.

IV. Conclusion

Motivation is the goal for any manager when creating an effective team. It is with this motivation that the journey can be enjoyed and the goal can be achieved. Motivation in staff is created by purpose and an understanding of how their work impacts the success of their team and organization. Through passion, mastery becomes possible and allows for progress, but all of this work means nothing without a core focus on Measurable Impact.

Measurable Impact is the difference between setting the goal and achieving the goal. Without a solid understanding of your progress and outcomes the work is aimless even if it comes with the best of intentions. The ingredients of purpose, mastery, and trust or autonomy when paired with Results-Based Accountability are important keys in a leader's quest for Measurable Impact, the Holy Grail of Public Leadership. If managers keep these elements in mind then they will be able to truly inspire others to join them on their journey.

[1] The key terms and their definitions come from Trying Hard is Not Good Enough by Mark Friedman.

[2] Hirsch, Sandra Krebs and Jean Kummerow. Introduction to Type and Organizations. 1993. CPP, Inc.

[3] Hirsch, Sandra Krebs and Jane Kise. Introduction to Type and Coaching, 2000, CPP, Inc.

[4] Schorr, L. B. (1998). Common purpose: Strengthening families and neighborhoods to rebuild America. New York, NY: Anchor Books.

[5] Kania, J., & Kramer, M., Collective impact. Stanford Social Innovation Review (9)1.
http://www.ssireview.org/articles/entry/collective_impact

[6] Pink, D. (2009). Drive: The surprising truth about what motivates us. New York, NY: Riverhead Books. 142.

[7] Pink, D. (2009). Drive: The surprising truth about what motivates us. New York, NY: Riverhead Books. 109.

[8] Gladwell, M. (2008). Outliers: The story of success. New York, NY: Back Bay Books/Little, Brown and Company. 40-79.

[9] Pink, D. (2009). Drive: The surprising truth about what motivates us. New York, NY: Riverhead Books. 125.

[10] Pink, D. (2009). Drive: The surprising truth about what motivates us. New York, NY: Riverhead Books. 127.

[11] Pink, D. (2009). Drive: The surprising truth about what motivates us. New York, NY: Riverhead Books. 97-98.

[12] Behn, R. D. (2001). Rethinking democratic accountability. Washington, DC: The Brookings Institute.

About the Author:

Adam Luecking, MPM
adam@ResultsLeadership.org

Adam Luecking, CEO of the Results Leadership Group, is also Board President of the Community Indicators Consortium and has previously served as a Senior Fellow at University of Maryland (UMD) Burns Academy of Leadership. He manages executive leadership programs, consulting services and technology deployment to agencies that serve children, families and communities.

Luecking also recently led the creation of the Results Scorecard, web-based software for Results-Based Accountability™ (RBA), that helps leaders in the public and nonprofit sectors accelerate the improvement of the quality of life in their communities and the performance of their agencies and programs.

Luecking earned his B.S. in International Business from the R.H. Smith School of Business and M.P.M. with a specialization in Leadership from the School of Public Policy at UMD. He has also studied at the Program on Negotiation at Harvard University and is a certified trainer in RBA and the Myers-Briggs Type Indicator.